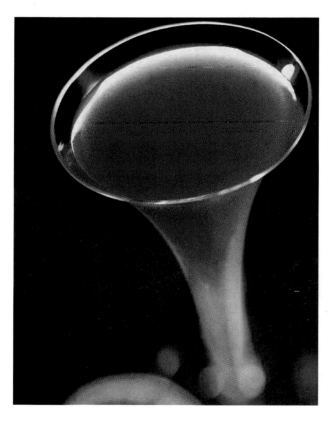

Cocktails

CLASSIC & CONTEMPORARY

Cocktails

THE ESSENTIAL COLLECTION

Linda Doeser

Photography by Chris Linton

p

This is a Parragon Publishing book
This edition published in 2004

Parragon Publishing
Queen Street House
4 Queen Street
Bath BA1 1HE, UK

Created and produced by
The Bridgewater Book Company

ISBN 1-40541-969-5

Printed in China

NOTE Recipes using uncooked eggs
should be avoided by infants, the elderly,
pregnant women, convalescents, and
anyone suffering from an illness.

Contents

introduction

Precisely where the word "cocktail" came from is uncertain. A popular piece of folklore describes how a Mexican princess called Xoctl offered a mixed drink to an American visitor to her father's court who confused her name with that of the drink itself. Another suggestion is that the spoon used for mixing drinks reminded imbibing racegoers of the docked tails of nonthoroughbred horses, called cocktails. There are many other flights of fancy, but modern etymologists mostly agree that the word derives from *coquetel*, a French, wine-based drink.

Whatever the origins of the word cocktail, mixed drinks have existed since ancient times and the first recognizable cocktail dates from about the sixteenth century. Indeed, many classics have been around for much longer than most people think. The bourbon-based Old Fashioned, for example, first

appeared at the end of the eighteenth century. We know that the word cocktail was already in use in 1809 in the United States and, thirty-five years later, when Charles Dickens described Major Pawkins as able to drink "more rum-toddy, mint-julep, gin-sling, and cock-tail, than any private gentleman of his acquaintance," it had reached Britain, too. Popular among the style-conscious and wealthy in the United States, cocktails were served before dinner in the most exclusive houses and hotels until World War I made them unfashionable. They have gone in and out of vogue ever since.

Following the war, young people, disillusioned by the elder generation and desperately seeking new experiences, pleasures, stimuli, and styles, developed a taste for a new range of cocktails. Ironically, Prohibition in the United States in the 1920s spurred on their development. Illegally produced liquor frequently tasted poisonous—and sometimes was—so its flavor needed to be disguised with fruit juices and mixers. No doubt, the naughtiness of drinking alcoholic cocktails also added to their appeal to the "bright young things" of the time. The craze quickly crossed the Atlantic and the best hotels in London, Paris, and Monte Carlo, where the quality of gin and whiskey was more consistent, soon boasted their own cocktail bars.

World War II brought an end to such revelry and, although drunk occasionally, cocktails remained out of style for decades until an exuberant renaissance in the 1970s. This resulted in another new generation of recipes, often featuring white rum and vodka, and tequila, which was just becoming known outside its native Mexico. Inevitably, the pendulum swung against cocktails again until recently. Now, once more, the cocktail shaker is essential equipment in every fashionable city bar.

essentials

Making, serving, and—above all—drinking cocktails should be fun. All you need is some basic equipment, a few ingredients, and a sense of adventure.

EQUIPMENT

Classic cocktails are either shaken or stirred. A shaker is an essential piece of equipment, consisting of a container with an inner, perforated lid and an outer lid. Both lids are secured while the mixture is shaken, together with cracked ice, and then the cocktail is strained through the perforated lid into a glass.

A mixing glass is a medium-size pitcher in which stirred cocktails can be mixed. It is usually made of uncolored glass so you can see what you are doing.

A long-handled bar spoon is perfect for stirring and a small strainer prevents the ice cubes—used during mixing—finding their way into the cocktail glass. Some modern cocktails, including slushes, are made in a blender or food processor, so if you have one, by all means make use of it. Any cocktail that is made by shaking can also be made in a blender.

Measuring cups, sometimes called "jiggers," and spoons are essential for getting the proportions right—guessing does not work. A corkscrew, bottle-opener, and sharp knife are crucial.

Other useful, but nonessential, tools include a citrus reamer, an ice bucket and tongs, a punch bowl, a glass serving pitcher, and a zester or grater. If you have a juicer, this is useful for making large quantities of fresh juice for cocktails, and for preparing a hangover cure the morning after!

GLASSES

You can serve cocktails in any glasses you like. Small, V-shaped, stemmed glasses may be worth buying, but it is not essential to have a full range of Old-fashioned, Highball, Collins glasses, and so on. Medium and straight-sided glasses and wine glasses cover most contingencies. As part of their appeal is visual, cocktails are best served in clear, uncut glass. Chill the glasses to ensure cocktails are cold.

INGREDIENTS

You can stock your bar over a period of time with the basics—it is not necessary to buy everything at once. A good selection of alcoholic drinks would include whiskey, possibly Scotch and bourbon, brandy, gin, light and dark rum, triple sec, sweet and dry vermouth, vodka, and tequila. You could also include Pernod, beer, and red and white wine. Keep champagne cocktails for special occasions. Select your stock according to your tastes —for example, if you never drink whiskey, it would be extravagant to buy Scotch, Irish, Canadian, American blended, and bourbon.

Standard mixers include club soda, sparkling mineral water, cola, ginger ale, and tonic water. Freshly squeezed juice is best, but when buying juice in a bottle or carton, avoid any with added sugar or extra "padding." Cranberry juice, for example, may be bulked with grape juice. Commercial brands of grapefruit, orange, cranberry, and tomato juices are useful.

A good supply of fresh lemons, limes, and oranges is essential. Fresh fruit is best, but if you use canned, buy it in natural juice rather than syrup, and drain well. Other useful decorations and condiments include Angostura bitters, Worcestershire sauce, and cocktail cherries. Finally, you can never have too much ice.

techniques

CRACKING AND CRUSHING ICE

Store ice in the freezer untll just before use. Cracked ice is used in both shaken and stirred cocktails. To crack ice, put ice cubes into a strong plastic bag and hit it against an outside wall, or put the ice between clean cloths on a sturdy counter and crush with a wooden mallet or rolling pin. Crushed ice is used in cocktails made in a blender. To crush ice, crack it as before but break it into much smaller pieces.

FROSTING GLASSES

Glasses can be frosted with sugar—or fine or coarse salt in the case of the Margarita. Simply rub the rim of the glass with a wedge of lemon or lime, then dip the rim into a saucer of superfine sugar or fine salt until it is coated.

MAKING SUGAR SYRUP

To make sugar syrup, put
4 tablespoons water and
4 tablespoons superfine sugar into a
small pan and stir over low heat
until the sugar has dissolved. Bring
to a boil, then continue to boil,
without stirring, for 1–2 minutes. Let
cool, then refrigerate in a covered
container for up to 2 weeks.

SHAKEN OR STIRRED?

To make a shaken cocktail, put fresh
cracked ice into a cocktail shaker and
pour over the other ingredients
immediately. Secure the lids and
shake vigorously for 10–20 seconds,
until the outside of the shaker is
coated in condensation. Strain into
a glass and serve at once. To make a
stirred cocktail, again use fresh
cracked ice and pour over the
ingredients immediately. Using a
long-handled spoon, stir vigorously,
without splashing, for 20 seconds,
then strain into a glass and serve
at once.

Classic Cocktails

classic
cocktail

... cannot lay claim to being the first
... even the only classic, but it has all
the characteristic hallmarks
of sophistication associated
with cocktails.

1 ... rim of a chilled cocktail
... a lemon wedge and dip in

2 ... pour brandy into a cocktail
... brandy, curaçao
... lemon juice over the ice
... vigorously until frost forms.

3 ... frosted glass and
decorate with a lemon twist.

Originally, boilermaker was American
slang for a shot of whiskey followed by a
beer chaser. This version is marginally
more sophisticated, but every bit as lethal.

boiler maker

- 1 cup
- 1½ mea

1

2

french 75

Although this cocktail was described in a cocktail recipe book written in the early twentieth century as something that "definitely hits the spot," there seems to be some confusion about the actual ingredients. All recipes include champagne, but disagree about the spirits included.

serves 1

- **4–6 cracked ice cubes**
- **2 measures brandy**
- **1 measure lemon juice**
- **1 tbsp sugar syrup (see page 15)**
- **chilled champagne, to top off**
- **twist of lemon peel, to decorate**

1 Put the cracked ice cubes into a cocktail shaker. Pour the brandy, lemon juice, and sugar syrup over the ice and shake vigorously until a frost forms.

2 Strain into a chilled highball glass and top off with champagne. Decorate the glass with the lemon twist.

b and b

Although elaborate concoctions are
great fun to mix—and drink—some
of the best cocktails are the
simplest. B and B—brandy and
Bénédictine—couldn't be easier, but
it has a superbly subtle flavor.

serves 1

- **4–6 cracked ice cubes**
- **1 measure brandy**
- **1 measure Bénédictine**

1 Put the cracked ice cubes into
a mixing glass. Pour the brandy
and Bénédictine over the ice
and stir to mix.

2 Strain into a chilled
cocktail glass.

corpse reviver

This cocktail is not designed to deal with a hangover the morning after, but it is a great pick-me-up after a busy day. Note that it will not prevent your needing a different kind of corpse reviver or some other sort of pick-me-up the next day. None of these cocktails comes with a medical guarantee.

serves 1

- 4–6 cracked ice cubes
- 2 measures brandy
- 1 measure apple brandy
- 1 measure sweet vermouth

1 Put the cracked ice cubes into a mixing glass. Pour the brandy, apple brandy, and vermouth over the ice. Stir gently to mix.

2 Strain into a chilled cocktail glass.

As the name of this cocktail always seems to imply romance and hints that the sheets in question are, at the very least, satin, make it for two people. Certainly, this delicious concoction is as smooth as silk.

between the
sheets

- 6 cracked ice cubes
- 2 measures brandy
- 2 measures white rum
- 1 measure clear Curaçao
- 1 measure lemon juice

1 Put the cracked ice cubes into a cocktail shaker. Pour the brandy, rum, Curaçao, and lemon juice over the ice. Shake vigorously until a frost forms.

2 Strain into two chilled wine glasses or goblets..

"A rose by any ot [...] "

1 [Put] the cracked ice c[ubes] [in a] shaker. Pour the brandy, gr[enadine, and] Pernod over the ice and add [...] Shake vigorously until a fro[...]

serves 1

- 4–6 cracked ice cubes

2 Strain into a chilled wine goblet and top up with sparkling wine. St[ir and] then decorate with the peach we[dge.]

- 1½ measures brandy
- 1 tsp grenadine
- ½ tsp Pernod
- ½ fresh peach, peeled and mashed
- sparkling wine, to top off
- fresh peach wedge, to decorate

brave
bull

Spain's historical association with Mexico has left many legacies—not least a taste for bullfighting—although whether this cocktail is named in tribute to the animal or because it makes the drinker proverbially brave is anyone's guess.

1   ice cubes into a
          the tequila and Tia
          and stir well to mix.

2   into a chilled goblet and
          with the spiral of lemon peel.

• spiral of lemon peel, to

cuba libre

- 4–6 cracked ice cubes
- 2 measures white rum
- cola, to top off
- wedge of lime, to decorate

The 1960s and 1970s saw the meteoric rise in popularity of this simple, long drink, perhaps because of highly successful marketing by Bacardi brand rum, the original white Cuban rum (now produced in the Bahamas), and Coca-Cola, but more likely because rum and cola seem to be natural companions.

1 Half fill a highball glass with cracked ice cubes. Pour the rum over the ice and top off with cola.

2 Stir gently to mix and decorate with a lime wedge.

zon

serves 1

...–6 crushed ice cubes

... measures dark rum

... measures white rum

... measure golden rum

... measure triple sec

... measure lime juice

... measure orange juice

... measure pineapple juice

... measure guava juice

... tbsp grenadine

... tbsp orgeat

... tsp Pernod

... sprig of fresh m...

... pineapple w...

... to decorat...

The individual ... ...
including liqu... ... ...
considerably f... ... ...
they all conta... ... ...
and dark rum ... ...

1 Put the crus... ... ...
add the three ru... ...
juice, pineapple ju... ...
orgeat, and Perno...

2 Pour, without stra... ...
Collins glass and decorate with the mint sprig
and pineapple wedges.

29

moscow
mule

This cocktail came into existence through
a happy coincidence during the 1930s.
An American bar owner had overstocked
ginger beer, and a representative of a
soft drinks company invented the
Moscow Mule to help him out.

serves 1

- **10–12 cracked ice cubes**
- **2 measures vodka**
- **1 measure lime juice**
- **ginger beer, to top off**
- **slice of lime, to decorate**

1 Put 4–6 cracked ice cubes into a cocktail
shaker. Pour the vodka and lime juice over
the ice. Shake vigorously until a frost forms.

2 Half fill a chilled highball glass with
cracked ice cubes and strain the cocktail over
them. Top off with ginger beer. Decorate with
a slice of lime.

rhett
butler

When Margaret Mitchell wrote her long civil war story, *Gone With the Wind*, she created an enduring romantic hero in Rhett Butler. His debonair charm and devil-may-care lifestyle were brought alive by the heart-throb film star Clark Gable.

serves 1

- **4–6 cracked ice cubes**
- **2 measures Southern Comfort**
- **½ measure clear Curaçao**
- **½ measure lime juice**
- **1 tsp lemon juice**
- **twist of lemon peel, to decorate**

1 Put the cracked ice cubes into a cocktail shaker. Pour the Southern Comfort, Curaçao, lime juice, and lemon juice over the ice. Shake vigorously until a frost forms.

2 Strain into a chilled cocktail glass and decorate with the lemon twist.

mint julep

A julep is simply a mixed drink sweetened with syrup—but the mere word conjures up images of ante-bellum cotton plantations and a long-gone, leisurely, and very gracious way of life.

serves 1

- **leaves of 1 fresh mint sprig**
- **1 tbsp sugar syrup (see page 15)**
- **6–8 crushed ice cubes**
- **3 measures bourbon whiskey**
- **fresh mint sprig, to decorate**

1 Put the mint leaves and sugar syrup into a small, chilled glass and mash with a teaspoon. Add crushed ice to fill the glass, then add the bourbon.

2 Decorate with the mint sprig.

Sours are short drinks, flavored with lemon or lime juice. They can be made with any spirit, although Whiskey Sour was the first and, for many, is still the favorite.

whiskey sour

serves 1

- **4–6 cracked ice cubes**

- **2 measures American blended whiskey**

- **1 measure lemon juice**

- **1 tsp sugar syrup (see page 15)**

- **cocktail cherry, slice of orange, to decorate**

1 Put the cracked ice cubes into a cocktail shaker. Pour the whiskey, lemon juice, and sugar syrup over the ice. Shake vigorously until a frost forms.

2 Strain into a chilled cocktail glass and decorate with the cherry and orange slice.

manhattan

Said to have been invented by Sir Winston
Churchill's American mother, the
Manhattan is one of the cocktails served at
places in New York. The smartest cocktail bars
in the Jazz Age, the Manhattan is back in fashion
with cocktail bars for a new generation.

serves 1

- **4–6 cracked ice cubes**
- **dash of Angostura bitters**
- **3 measures rye whiskey**
- **1 measure sweet vermouth**
- **cocktail cherry,
  to decorate**

1 Put the cracked ice cubes into a
mixing glass. Dash the Angostura
bitters over the ice and pour in the
whiskey and vermouth. Stir well
to mix.

2 Strain into a chilled glass and
decorate with the cherry.

Simple, elegant, subtle, and much more powerful

than appearance suggests, this is the perfect

cocktail to serve before an al fresco summer dinner.

white lady

serves 1

- **4–6 cracked ice cubes**
- **2 measures gin**
- **1 measure triple sec**
- **1 measure lemon juice**

1 Put the cracked ice cubes into a
cocktail shaker. Pour the gin, triple sec,
and lemon juice over the ice. Shake
vigorously until a frost forms.

2 Strain into a chilled cocktail glass.

This creamy, chocolate-flavored, gin-based cocktail, decorated with grated nutmeg, is the head of an extended family of cocktails, which continues to grow.

alexander

serves 1

- **4–6 cracked ice cubes**
- **1 measure gin**
- **1 measure crème de cacao**
- **1 measure light cream**
- **freshly grated nutmeg, to decorate**

1 Put the cracked ice cubes into a cocktail shaker. Pour the gin, crème de cacao, and light cream over the ice. Shake vigorously until a frost forms.

2 Strain into a chilled cocktail glass and sprinkle with the nutmeg.

tom collins

This cocktail combines gin, lemon juice, and club soda to make a cooling long drink. This is a venerable cocktail, but the progenitor of several generations of the Collins family of drinks, scattered across the globe, was the popular John Collins cocktail.

serves 1

- **5–6 cracked ice cubes**
- **3 measures gin**
- **2 measures lemon juice**
- **½ measure sugar syrup (see page 15)**
- **club soda, to top off**
- **slice of lemon, to decorate**

1 Put the cracked ice cubes into a cocktail shaker. Pour the gin, lemon juice, and sugar syrup over the ice. Shake vigorously until a frost forms.

2 Strain into a tall, chilled glass and top off with club soda. Decorate the glass with a slice of lemon.

It is disappointing to discover that the pretty
name of this cocktail is derived from the
practice of adding fresh orange juice to bathtub
gin during the years of Prohibition in the United
States in order to conceal its filthy flavor. Made
with good-quality gin, which needs no such
concealment, it is delightfully refreshing.

orange
blossom

serves 1

- **4–6 cracked ice cubes**
- **2 measures gin**
- **2 measures orange juice**
- **slice of orange,
  to decorate**

1 Put the cracked ice cubes into
a cocktail shaker. Pour the gin and
orange juice over the ice and shake
vigorously until a frost forms.

2 Strain into a chilled cocktail glass
and decorate with the orange slice.

old fashioned

So ubiquitous is this cocktail that a small, straight-sided tumbler is known as an Old Fashioned glass. It is a perfect illustration of the saying, "Sometimes the old ones are the best."

serves 1

- sugar cube
- dash of Angostura bitters
- 1 tsp water
- 2 measures bourbon or rye whiskey
- 4–6 cracked ice cubes
- twist of lemon peel, to decorate

1 Place the sugar cube in a small, chilled Old Fashioned glass. Dash the bitters over the cube and add the water. Mash with a spoon until the sugar has dissolved.

2 Pour the bourbon or rye whiskey into the glass and stir. Add the cracked ice cubes and decorate with the lemon twist.

For many, this is the ultimate cocktail. It is named after its inventor, Martini de Anna de Toggia, and not the famous brand of vermouth. The original version comprised equal measures of gin and vermouth, now known as a Fifty-Fifty, but the proportions vary, up to the Ultra Dry Martini, when the glass is merely rinsed out with vermouth before the gin is poured in.

serves 1

• 4–6 cracked ice cubes

• 3 measures gin

• 1 tsp dry vermouth, or to taste

• cocktail olive, to decorate

martini

1 Put the cracked ice cubes into a mixing glass. Pour the gin and vermouth over the ice and stir well to mix.

2 Strain into a chilled cocktail glass and decorate with a cocktail olive.

singapore
sling

In the days of the British Empire, the privileged would gather in the relative cool of the evening to refresh parched throats and gossip about the day's events at exclusive clubs. Those days are long gone, but a Singapore Sling is still the ideal thirst-quencher on hot summer evenings.

serves 1

- • 10–12 cracked ice cubes
- • 2 measures gin
- • 1 measure cherry brandy
- • 1 measure lemon juice
- • 1 tsp grenadine
- • club soda, to top off
- • lime peel, cocktail cherries, to decorate

1 Put 4–6 cracked ice cubes into a cocktail shaker. Pour the gin, cherry brandy, lemon juice, and grenadine over the ice. Shake vigorously until a frost forms.

2 Half fill a chilled highball glass with cracked ice cubes and strain the cocktail over them. Top off with club soda and decorate with lime peel and cocktail cherries.

The name of this cocktail aptly
describes its pretty color. Too many,
however, and maidenly modesty may
be abandoned and blushing could
become compulsory.

maiden's blush

serves 1

4–6 cracked ice cubes

2 measures gin

½ tsp triple sec

½ tsp grenadine

½ tsp lemon juice

1 Put the cracked ice cubes into a
cocktail shaker. Pour the gin, triple sec,
grenadine, and lemon juice over the ice.
Shake vigorously until a frost forms.

2 Strain into a chilled cocktail glass
or small highball glass.

piña colada

One of the younger generation of classics, this became popular during the cocktail revival of the 1980s and has remained so ever since.

serves 1

- **4–6 crushed ice cubes**
- **2 measures white rum**
- **1 measure dark rum**
- **3 measures pineapple juice**
- **2 measures coconut cream**
- **pineapple wedges, to decorate**

1 Put the crushed ice cubes into a blender and add the white rum, dark rum, pineapple juice, and coconut cream. Blend until smooth.

2 Pour, without straining, into a tall, chilled glass and decorate with pineapple wedges speared on a cocktail stick.

daiquiri

Daiquiri is a town in Cuba, where this drink was said to have been invented in the early part of the twentieth century. A businessman had run out of imported gin and so had to make do with the local drink—rum—which, at that time, was of unreliable quality. To ensure that his guests would find it palatable he mixed it with other ingredients. This classic has since given rise to almost innumerable variations.

serves 1

- 4–6 cracked ice cubes
- 2 measures white rum
- 3/4 measure lime juice
- 1/2 tsp sugar syrup (see page 15)

1 Put the cracked ice cubes into a cocktail shaker. Pour the rum, lime juice, and sugar syrup over the ice. Shake vigorously until a frost forms.

2 Strain into a chilled cocktail glass.

Derived from a Hindi word meaning five, punch is

so called because, traditionally, it contained five

ingredients. These should also include

four basic flavors—

strong, weak, sour,

and sweet.

plan
pun

serves 1

- 10–12 cracked ice cubes
- dash of grenadine
- 2 measures white rum
- 2 measures dark rum
- 1 measure lemon juice
- 1 measure lime juice
- 1 tsp sugar syrup (see page 15)
- ¼ tsp triple sec
- sparkling mineral water,
  to top off
- slice of lemon,
  slice of lime,
  slice of pineapple,
  cocktail cherry, to decorate

...ues into a
...grenadine
...pour in the white
rum, dark rum, lemon juice, lime
juice, sugar syrup, and triple sec.
Shake vigorously until a frost forms.

Half fill a tall, chilled Collins
glass with cracked ice cubes and
strain the cocktail over them. Top off
with sparkling mineral water and stir.
Decorate with the lemon, lime, and
pineapple slices, and a cherry.

margarita

The traditional way to drink tequila is to shake a little salt on the back of your hand between the thumb and forefinger and, holding a wedge of lime or lemon, lick the salt, suck the fruit, and then down a shot of tequila in one. This cocktail, attributed to Francisco Morales and invented in 1942 in Mexico, is a more civilized version.

serves 1

- **lime wedge**
- **coarse salt**
- **4–6 cracked ice cubes**
- **3 measures white tequila**
- **1 measure triple sec**
- **2 measures lime juice**
- **slice of lime, to decorate**

1 Rub the rim of a chilled cocktail glass with the lime wedge and then dip in a saucer of coarse salt to frost.

2 Put the cracked ice cubes into a cocktail shaker. Pour the tequila, triple sec, and lime juice over the ice. Shake vigorously until a frost forms.

3 Strain into the prepared glass and decorate with the lime slice.

... so that you shouldn't rush
this mixing, otherwise you will spoil
the attractive sunrise effect as the
grenadine slowly spreads through the
orange juice.

tequila sunrise

serves...

• 4–6 cracked ice cubes

• 2 parts...tequila

orange juice...

• 1 measure...

Put the cracked ice cubes into a
chilled highball glass. Pour the tequila
over the ice and top off with the
orange juice. Stir well to mix...

...add the grenadine...

bloody mary

This classic cocktail was invented in 1921 at the legendary Harry's Bar in Paris. There are numerous versions—some much hotter and spicier than others. Ingredients may include horseradish sauce in addition to or instead of Tabasco sauce, more or less tomato juice, and lime juice instead of lemon. Sometimes the glass is decorated with a sprig of mint. Whatever the version, all experts agree that it is essential to use the highest-quality ingredients.

serves 1

- **4–6 cracked ice cubes**
- **dash of Worcestershire sauce**
- **dash of Tabasco sauce**
- **2 measures vodka**
- **6 measures tomato juice**
- **juice of ½ lemon**
- **pinch of celery salt**
- **pinch of cayenne pepper**
- **celery stalk with leaves, slice of lemon, to decorate**

1 Put the cracked ice into a cocktail shaker. Dash the Worcestershire sauce and Tabasco sauce over the ice and pour in the vodka, tomato juice, and lemon juice. Shake vigorously until a frost forms.

2 Strain into a tall, chilled glass, add a pinch of celery salt and a pinch of cayenne, and decorate with a celery stalk and a slice of lemon.

History records only White and Red Russians. The omission of the Black Russian is a sad oversight. For a coffee liqueur, you can use either Tia Maria or Kahlúa, depending on your personal taste—the latter is sweeter.

black russian

serves 1

• 4–6 cracked ice cubes

• 2 measures vodka

• 1 measure coffee liqueur

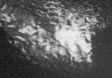

1 Put the cracked ice into a small, chilled highball glass. Pour the vodka and liqueur over the ice. Stir to mix.

49

screwdriver

Always use freshly squeezed orange juice to make this refreshing cocktail—it is just not the same with bottled juice. This simple, classic cocktail has given rise to numerous and increasingly elaborate variations.

serves 1

• 6–8 cracked ice cubes

• 2 measures vodka

• orange juice, to top off

• slice of orange,
to decorate

1 Fill a chilled highball glass with cracked ice cubes. Pour the vodka over the ice and top off with orange juice.

2 Stir well to mix and decorate with a slice of orange.

A popular cocktail ingredient, the *digestif* absinthe is no longer available. Flavored with wormwood, which is said to react with alcohol to cause brain damage, absinthe was banned by law in 1915. However, various pastis, including Pernod and Ricard, are still available and make good substitutes.

absinthe friend

serves 1

- 4–6 cracked ice cubes
- dash of Angostura bitters
- dash of sugar syrup (see page 15)
- 1 measure Pernod
- 1 measure gin

1 Put the cracked ice cubes into a cocktail shaker. Dash the bitters and sugar syrup over the ice and pour in the Pernod and gin. Shake vigorously until a frost forms.

2 Strain into a chilled glass.

51

negroni

This aristocratic cocktail was created
by Count Negroni at the Bar Giacosa
in Florence, although since then,
the proportions of gin to Campari
have altered.

serves 1

- **4–6 cracked ice cubes**
- **1 measure Campari**
- **1 measure gin**
- **½ measure sweet vermouth**
- **twist of orange peel,
  to decorate**

1 Put the cracked ice cubes into a
mixing glass. Pour the Campari, gin, and
vermouth over the ice. Stir well to mix.

2 Strain into a chilled glass and
decorate with the orange twist.

Hardly surprisingly, several classic cocktails have been named after this classic marque. This version was created by author H. E. Bates in his popular novel *The Darling Buds of May*.

rolls royce

serves 1

- **4–6 cracked ice cubes**
- **dash of orange bitters**
- **2 measures dry vermouth**
- **1 measure dry gin**
- **1 measure Scotch whisky**

1 Put the cracked ice cubes into a mixing glass. Dash the bitters over the ice.

2 Pour the vermouth, gin, and whisky over the ice and stir to mix. Strain into a chilled cocktail glass.

kir

As with the best mustard, crème de cassis production is centered on the French city of Dijon. This cocktail is named in commemoration of a partisan and mayor of the city, Félix Kir.

serves 1

- 4–6 crushed ice cubes
- 2 measures crème de cassis
- white wine, to top off
- twist of lemon peel, to decorate

1 Put the crushed ice cubes into a chilled wine glass. Pour the crème de cassis over the ice.

2 Top off with chilled white wine and stir well. Decorate with the lemon twist.

A long drink made with syrup and fresh fruit decorations, Sherry Cobbler is the original, but there are now numerous and often more potent variations.

sherry cobbler

serves 1

- **6–8 crushed ice cubes**
- **¼ tsp sugar syrup (see page 15)**
- **¼ tsp clear Curaçao**
- **4 measures Amontillado sherry**
- **pineapple wedges, twist of lemon peel, to decorate**

1 Fill a wine glass with crushed ice cubes. Add the sugar syrup and Curaçao and stir gently until a frost forms.

2 Pour in the sherry and stir well. Decorate with pineapple wedges speared on a cocktail stick and the lemon twist.

acapulco

This is one of many cocktails that has changed from its original recipe over the years. To start with, it was always rum-based and did not include any fruit juice. Nowadays, it is increasingly made with tequila, because this has become better known outside its native Mexico.

serves 1

- **10–12 cracked ice cubes**
- **2 measures white rum**
- **½ measure triple sec**
- **½ measure lime juice**
- **1 tsp sugar syrup (see page 15)**
- **1 egg white**
- **sprig of fresh mint, to decorate**

1 Put 4–6 cracked ice cubes into a cocktail shaker. Pour the rum, triple sec, lime juice, and sugar syrup over the ice and add the egg white. Shake vigorously until a frost forms.

2 Half fill a chilled highball glass with cracked ice cubes and strain the cocktail over them. Decorate with the mint sprig.

Cointreau is the best-known brand of the orange-flavored liqueur known generically as triple sec. It is drier and stronger than Curaçao and is always colorless.

sidecar

serves 1

• 4–6 cracked ice cubes

• 2 measures brandy

• 1 measure triple sec

• 1 measure lemon juice

• twist of orange peel to decorate

1

2

bronx

Like Manhattan, the New York borough of the Bronx—and also the river of the same name—have been immortalized in cocktail bars throughout the world.

serves 1

1 cracked ice cubes

1 Put the cracked ice cubes into a mixing glass. Pour the gin, orange juice, dry and sweet vermouth over the ice and stir to mix.

2 Strain into a chilled cocktail glass.

buck's fizz

Invented at Buck's Club in London, the
original was invariably made with
Bollinger champagne and it is true that
the better the quality of the champagne,
the better the flavor.

serves 1

• **2 measures chilled champagne**

• **2 measures chilled orange juice**

1 Pour the champagne into a chilled
champagne flute, then pour in the
orange juice.

Contemporary Cocktails

highland fling

Blended whisky is best suited to cocktails—single malts should always be drunk neat or simply with a little added mineral water. However, a throat-burning, harsh blend will make a mixture closer to rocket fuel than a cocktail and no amount of additional flavors will improve it.

serves 1

- 4–6 cracked ice cubes
- dash of Angostura bitters
- 2 measures Scotch whisky
- 1 measure sweet vermouth
- cocktail olive, to decorate

1 Put the cracked ice cubes into a mixing glass. Dash Angostura bitters over the ice. Pour the whisky and vermouth over the ice.

2 Stir well to mix and strain into a chilled glass. Decorate with a cocktail olive.

Slivovitz is a colorless plum brandy, usually made from Mirabelle and Switzen plums. It is usually drunk straight, but can add a fruity note to cocktails. If it is not available, you could substitute apricot, peach, or cherry brandy—all fruits from the same family—but the cocktail will not look or taste quite the same.

panda

serves 1

- **4–6 cracked ice cubes**
- **dash of sugar syrup (see page 15)**
- **1 measure slivovitz**
- **1 measure apple brandy**
- **1 measure gin**
- **1 measure orange juice**

1 Put the cracked ice cubes into a cocktail shaker. Dash the sugar syrup over the ice and pour in the slivovitz, apple brandy, gin, and orange juice. Shake vigorously until a frost forms.

2 Strain into a chilled cocktail glass.

twin peaks

Bourbon, named after a county in Kentucky, must be made from at least 51 percent corn mash and is America's most popular whiskey. It forms the basis of many more cocktails than its Scotch cousin.

serves 1

- 4–6 cracked ice cubes
- dash of triple sec
- 2 measures bourbon
- 1 measure Bénédictine
- 1 measure lime juice
- slice of lime, to decorate

1 Put the cracked ice cubes into a cocktail shaker. Dash triple sec over the ice and pour in the bourbon, Bénédictine, and lime juice. Shake vigorously until a frost forms.

2 Strain into a chilled highball glass and decorate with a slice of lime.

A shillelagh (pronounced *shee-lay-lee*) is a wooden cudgel, traditionally made from blackthorn. Undoubtedly, this is a cocktail that hits the spot.

irish shillelagh

serves 1

- **4–6 crushed ice cubes**
- **2 measures Irish whiskey**
- **1 measure lemon juice**
- **1/2 measure sloe gin**
- **1/2 measure white rum**
- **1/2 tsp sugar syrup (see page 15)**
- **1/2 peach, peeled, pitted, and finely chopped**
- **2 raspberries, to decorate**

1 Put the crushed ice cubes into a blender and add the whiskey, lemon juice, sloe gin, rum, sugar syrup, and chopped peach. Blend until smooth.

2 Pour into a small, chilled highball glass and decorate with raspberries.

adam's
apple

Applejack in the United States, Calvados in France and apple brandy as a generic term—whatever you call it, it provides a delicious fruity flavor and a tempting aroma to this cocktail.

serves 1

- **4–6 cracked ice cubes**
- **dash of yellow Chartreuse**
- **2 measures apple brandy**
- **1 measure gin**
- **1 measure dry vermouth**

1 Put the cracked ice cubes into a mixing glass. Dash the Chartreuse over the ice and pour in the apple brandy, gin, and vermouth.

2 Stir well to mix, then strain into a chilled glass.

A powerful mix, this cocktail is more likely to
fire you into orbit than to reduce you to trying
to rake the moon's reflection out of a pond.

moonraker

serves 1

- 4–6 cracked ice cubes
- dash of Pernod
- 1 measure brandy
- 1 measure peach brandy
- 1 measure quinquina

1 Put the cracked ice cubes into a mixing
glass. Dash Pernod over the ice and pour in
the brandy, peach brandy, and quinquina.

2 Stir well to mix, then strain into a
chilled highball glass.

cowboy

In movies, cowboys drink their rye straight, often

pulling the cork out of the bottle with their teeth,

and it is certainly difficult to imagine John Wayne

or Clint Eastwood sipping delicately from a

chilled cocktail glass.

serves 1

• **4–6 cracked ice cubes**

• **3 measures rye whiskey**

• **2 tbsp light cream**

1 Put the cracked ice cubes into a cocktail shaker. Pour the whiskey and cream over the ice. Shake vigorously until a frost forms.

2 Strain into a chilled highball glass.

A cat's eye is many things—apart from what a cat sees with—including a semiprecious stone and a stripy marble. Now, it's a highly potent cocktail, as pretty as a gemstone and certainly more fun than playing marbles.

cat's eye

serves 1

- **4–6 cracked ice cubes**
- **2 measures gin**
- **1½ measures dry vermouth**
- **½ measure Kirsch**
- **½ measure triple sec**
- **½ measure lemon juice**
- **½ measure water**

1 Put the cracked ice cubes into a cocktail shaker. Pour the gin, vermouth, Kirsch, triple sec, lemon juice, and water over the ice.

2 Shake vigorously until a frost forms. Strain into a chilled goblet.

breakfast

It is difficult to believe that anyone
would actually have the stomach to cope
with cocktails first thing in the morning
—but then, for those who party all night
and sleep all day, cocktail time coincides
with breakfast.

serves 1

• 4–6 cracked ice cubes

• 2 measures gin

• 1 measure grenadine

• 1 egg yolk

1 Put the cracked ice cubes into a
cocktail shaker. Pour the gin and
grenadine over the ice and add the egg
yolk. Shake vigorously until a frost forms.

2 Strain into a chilled highball glass.

You will have to make up
your own mind whether
this cocktail is a cure for
someone already suffering
or whether it is the cause of
suffering still to come.

suffering fool

serves 1

- 1 tbsp Angostura bitters

- 6–8 cracked ice cubes

- 2 measures gin

- 1½ measures brandy

- ½ measure lime juice

- 1 tsp sugar syrup (see page 15)

- ginger beer, to top off

- slice each of cucumber and lime,
  sprig of fresh mint,
  to decorate

1 Pour the Angostura bitters into a chilled Collins glass and swirl round until the inside of the glass is coated. Pour out the excess and discard.

2 Half fill the glass with cracked ice cubes. Pour the gin, brandy, lime juice, and sugar syrup over the ice. Stir well to mix.

3 Top off with ginger beer and stir gently. Decorate with the cucumber and lime slices and a mint sprig.

This is a truly spectacular cocktail and can be great fun to decorate. Look out for swizzle sticks in the shape of palm trees or hula dancers and elaborately curly straws.

coco loco

serves 1

- 1 fresh coconut
- 8–10 crushed ice cubes
- 2 measures white tequila
- 1 measure gin
- 1 measure white rum
- 2 measures pineapple juice
- 1 tsp sugar syrup (see page 15)
- ½ lime

1 Carefully saw the top off the coconut, reserving the liquid inside.

2 Add the crushed ice, tequila, gin, rum, pineapple juice, and sugar syrup to the coconut, together with the reserved coconut liquid.

3 Squeeze the lime over the cocktail and drop it in. Stir well and serve with a straw.

vodga

As a rule, classic cocktails based on vodka were intended to provide the kick of an alcoholic drink with no tell-tale signs on the breath and they were usually fairly simple mixes of fruit juice, sodas, and other nonalcoholic flavorings. By contrast, contemporary cocktails based on vodka often include other aromatic and flavorsome spirits and liqueurs, with vodka adding extra strength.

serves 1

- **4–6 cracked ice cubes**
- **2 measures vodka**
- **1 measure Strega**
- **½ measure orange juice**

1 Put the cracked ice cubes into a cocktail shaker. Pour the vodka, Strega, and orange juice over the ice. Shake vigorously until a frost forms.

2 Strain into a chilled cocktail glass.

nirvana

It may not be possible to obtain a perfect state of harmony and bliss through a cocktail, but this has to be the next best thing.

serves 1

- **8–10 cracked ice cubes**
- **2 measures dark rum**
- **½ measure grenadine**
- **½ measure tamarind syrup**
- **1 tsp sugar syrup (see page 15)**
- **grapefruit juice, to top off**

1 Put 4–6 cracked ice cubes into a cocktail shaker. Pour the rum, grenadine, tamarind syrup, and sugar syrup over the ice and shake vigorously until a frost forms.

2 Half fill a chilled Collins glass with cracked ice cubes and strain the cocktail over them. Top off with grapefruit juice.

If the fairy-story heroine had been knocking back cocktails until the clock struck midnight, it's hardly surprising that she forgot the time, mislaid her pumpkin, and lost her shoe on the way home.

cinderella

serves 1

- **4–6 cracked ice cubes**
- **3 measures white rum**
- **1 measure white port**
- **1 measure lemon juice**
- **1 tsp sugar syrup (see page 15)**
- **1 egg white**

1 Put the cracked ice cubes into a cocktail shaker. Pour the rum, port, lemon juice, and sugar syrup over the ice and add the egg white.

2 Shake vigorously until a frost forms and strain into a chilled glass.

palm beach

If it's been a long time since your last
holiday, conjure up the blue skies and
the rolling surf of Florida with this
sunny cocktail.

serves 1

- **4–6 cracked ice cubes**
- **1 measure white rum**
- **1 measure gin**
- **1 measure pineapple juice**

1 Put the cracked ice cubes into a
cocktail shaker. Pour the rum, gin, and
pineapple juice over the ice. Shake
vigorously until a frost forms.

2 Strain into a chilled glass.

One or two Diablos and you will
certainly feel a bit of a devil, but one
or two too many and you will feel like
the very devil.

el diablo

serves 1

- 6–8 cracked ice cubes
- 2–3 strips of lime peel
- 1 measure lime juice
- 3 measures white tequila
- 1 measure crème de cassis

1 Fill a highball glass with cracked
ice cubes and add the lime peel.

2 Pour the lime juice over the ice, then
add the tequila and crème de cassis.

huatusco
whammer

To be authentic, this cocktail should be topped
up with Coca-Cola, but you can use other brands
of cola if you prefer. Make sure that the cola is
well chilled.

serves 1

- 8–10 cracked ice cubes
- 1 measure white tequila
- ½ measure white rum
- ½ measure vodka
- ½ measure gin
- ½ measure triple sec
- 1 measure lemon juice
- ½ tsp sugar syrup (see page 15)
- cola, to top off

1 Put 4–6 cracked ice cubes into a
cocktail shaker. Pour the tequila, rum,
vodka, gin, triple sec, lemon juice, and
sugar syrup over the ice. Shake
vigorously until a frost forms.

2 Fill a chilled Collins glass with
cracked ice cubes and strain the
cocktail over them. Top off with cola,
stir gently, and serve with straws.

78

In spite of the horrible literary pun in the name, this popular cocktail is fast becoming a modern classic.

tequila
mockingbird

serves 1

- 4–6 cracked ice cubes
- 2 measures white tequila
- 1 measure white crème de menthe

1 measure fresh lime juice

1 Put the cracked ice cubes into a cocktail shaker. Add the tequila, crème de menthe, and lime juice. Shake vigorously until a frost forms.

2 Strain into a chilled glass.

wild night out

Tequila has a reputation for being an extraordinarily potent spirit, but most commercially exported brands are the same standard strength as other spirits, such as gin or whiskey. "Home-grown" tequila or its close relative, mescal, may be quite another matter.

serves 1

- 4–6 cracked ice cubes
- 3 measures white tequila
- 2 measures cranberry juice
- 1 measure lime juice
- club soda, to top off

1 Put the cracked ice cubes into a cocktail shaker. Pour the tequila, cranberry juice, and lime juice over the ice. Shake vigorously until a frost forms.

2 Half fill a chilled highball glass with cracked ice cubes and strain the cocktail over them. Add club soda to taste.

White tequila is most commonly used for mixing cocktails, but some require the mellower flavor of the amber-colored, aged tequilas, which are known as golden tequila or *añejo*.

carolina

serves 1

- **4–6 cracked ice cubes**
- **3 measures golden tequila**
- **1 tsp grenadine**
- **1 tsp vanilla extract**
- **1 measure light cream**
- **1 egg white**
- **ground cinnamon, cocktail cherry, to decorate**

1 Put the cracked ice cubes into a cocktail shaker. Pour the tequila, grenadine, vanilla, and cream over the ice and add the egg white. Shake vigorously until a frost forms.

2 Strain into a chilled cocktail glass. Sprinkle with cinnamon and decorate with a cocktail cherry.

what the hell

Cheer yourself up when you are at a loose end, or when everything seems to have gone wrong, with this simple but delicious concoction.

serves 1

- **4–6 cracked ice cubes**
- **dash of lime juice**
- **1 measure gin**
- **1 measure apricot brandy**
- **1 measure dry vermouth**
- **twist of lemon peel, to decorate**

1 Put the cracked ice cubes into a mixing glass. Dash the lime juice over the ice and pour in the gin, apricot brandy, and vermouth. Stir well to mix.

2 Strain into a chilled cocktail glass and decorate with a twist of lemon peel.

An irresistible melding of perfect partners—rum, cherry, chocolate, and cream—this cocktail is almost too good to be true.

hayden's milk float

1 Put the cracked ice cubes into a cocktail shaker. Pour the rum, Kirsch, crème de cacao, and cream over the ice. Shake vigorously until a frost forms.

2 Strain into a chilled highball glass. Sprinkle with grated chocolate and decorate with a cocktail cherry.

serves 1

- **4–6 cracked ice cubes**
- **2 measures white rum**
- **1 measure Kirsch**
- **1 measure white crème de cacao**
- **1 measure light cream**
- **grated chocolate, cocktail cherry, to decorate**

crocodile

This is certainly a snappy cocktail with a bit of a bite. However, it probably gets its name from its spectacular color—Midori, a Japanese melon-flavored liqueur, is a startling shade of green.

serves 1

- 4–6 cracked ice cubes
- 2 measures vodka
- 1 measure triple sec
- 1 measure Midori
- 2 measures lemon juice

1 Put the cracked ice cubes into a cocktail shaker. Pour the vodka, triple sec, Midori, and lemon juice over the ice. Shake vigorously until a frost forms.

2 Strain into a chilled cocktail glass.

82

This is another one of those cocktails with a name that plays on the ingredients—fuzzy to remind you that it contains peach schnapps and navel because it is mixed with orange juice. It is no reflection on anyone's personal hygiene.

fuzzy navel

serves 1

- 4–6 cracked ice cubes
- 2 measures vodka
- 1 measure peach schnapps
- 1 cup orange juice
- slice of orange, to decorate

1

2

85

mudslide

This rather ominous-sounding cocktail is
actually a gorgeously creamy and richly
flavored concoction that is delicious
whatever the weather conditions.

serves 1

- 4–6 cracked ice cubes
- 1½ measures Kahlúa
- 1½ measures Bailey's Irish Cream
- 1½ measures vodka

1 Put the cracked ice cubes into a
cocktail shaker. Pour the Kahlúa,
Bailey's Irish Cream, and vodka over the
ice. Shake vigorously until a frost forms.

2 Strain into a chilled goblet.

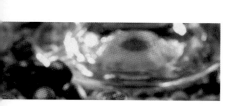

Amaretto is an Italian liqueur, so perhaps the inspiration for this cocktail comes from Don Corleone, the eponymous character in Mario Puzo's best-selling novel, unforgettably portrayed in the film by Marlon Brando.

godfather

serves 1

- **4–6 cracked ice cubes**
- **2 measures Scotch whisky**
- **1 measure amaretto**

1 Fill a chilled highball glass with cracked ice cubes. Pour in the whisky and amaretto and stir to mix.

It would probably be unwise to
investigate the provenance of this oddly
named cocktail—perhaps it is so called

bosom
caresser

serves 1

- **4–6 cracked ice cubes**

- **dash of triple sec**

- **1 measure brandy**

- **1 measure Madeira**

1 Put the cracked ice cubes into a
mixing glass. Dash triple sec over the
ice and pour in the brandy and Madeira.

2 Stir well to mix, then strain into a
chilled cocktail glass.

bishop

It is strange how men of the cloth have gained a reputation for being enthusiastic about the good, material things in life. Even Rudyard Kipling wrote about smuggling "brandy for the parson." It goes to show that spirituality is no barrier to spirits.

serves 1

- 4–6 cracked ice cubes
- dash of lemon juice
- 1 measure white rum
- 1 tsp red wine
- pinch of superfine sugar

1 Put the cracked ice cubes into a cocktail shaker. Dash the lemon juice over the ice, pour in the white rum and red wine, and add a pinch of sugar. Shake vigorously until a frost forms.

2 Strain into a chilled wine glass.

freedom
fighter

Crème Yvette is an American liqueur flavored
with Parma violets. As it has such a distinctive
taste, you either love it or hate it—but it certainly
makes pretty cocktails because it is such a lovely
color. You could also use crème de violette, which
is similar although not identical.

serves 1

• 4–6 cracked ice cubes

• 3 measures sloe gin

• 1 measure Crème Yvette

• 1 measure lemon juice

• 1 egg white

1 Put the cracked ice cubes
into a cocktail shaker. Pour
the gin, Crème Yvette, and lemon
juice over the ice and add the
egg white. Shake vigorously until
a frost forms.

2 Strain into a chilled wine glass.

A surprising number of cocktails are named after ghouls, ghosts, and things that go bump in the night. It seems unlikely that this one will get you wailing (except with delight), but it might make your hair stand on end.

banshee

serves 1

- 4–6 cracked ice cubes
- 2 measures crème de banane
- 1 measure crème de cacao
- 1 measure light cream

1 Put the cracked ice cubes into a cocktail shaker. Pour the crème de banane, crème de cacao, and light cream over the ice. Shake vigorously until a frost forms.

2 Strain into a chilled wine glass.

angel's
delight

This is a modern version of the classic
pousse café, an unmixed, mixed drink, in
that the ingredients form separate layers
in the glass—providing a ...
hand—...
drink...
more ...

serves 1

- ½ measure chilled grenadine
- ½ measure chilled triple sec
- ½ measure chilled sloe gin
- ½ measure chilled light cream

1 Pour the grenadine into a chilled
shot glass, pousse café glass, or
champagne flute, then, with a steady
hand, pour in the triple sec to make a
second layer.

2 Add the sloe gin to make a third
layer and, finally, add the cream to
float on top.

The expression "full monty," meaning not holding anything back, has been around for a long time, but was given a new lease of life by the highly successful British film of the same title. However, you can keep your clothes on when mixing and drinking this cocktail, but you might want to take them off when you've had a couple.

full monty

serves 1

- 4–6 cracked ice cubes
- 1 measure vodka
- 1 measure Galliano
- grated ginseng root, to decorate

1 Put the cracked ice cubes into a cocktail shaker. Pour the vodka and Galliano over the ice. Shake vigorously until a frost forms.

2 Strain into a chilled cocktail glass and sprinkle with grated ginseng root.

chile willy

Truly a cocktail for the brave-hearted—the heat depends on the type of chile, because some are much more fiery than others, as well as the quantity you add and whether the chile was seeded first. For an even spicier cocktail, use chili vodka instead of plain.

serves 1

- 4–6 cracked ice cubes
- 2 measures vodka
- 1 tsp chopped fresh chile

1 Put the ice into a cocktail shaker. Pour the vodka over the ice and add the chile.

2 Shake until a frost forms and strain into a chilled glass.

pink
squirrel

Crème de noyaux
has a wonderful,
slightly bitter, nutty
flavor, but is, in fact,
made from peach and
apricot pits. It is usually
served as a liqueur, but does
combine well with some
other ingredients in cocktails.

serves 1

- **4–6 cracked ice cubes**
- **2 measures dark crème de cacao**
- **1 measure crème de noyaux**
- **1 measure light cream**

1 Put the cracked ice cubes into a cocktail shaker. Pour the crème de cacao, crème de noyaux, and light cream over the ice. Shake vigorously until a frost forms.

2 Strain into a chilled cocktail glass.

starbangled
spanner

Although only half measures of each spirit are used, there are seven layers of them, so this is quite a potent cocktail. It is probably fortunate that after getting your tongue round a couple, your hand will become too unsteady to pour more.

1 Pour the green Chartreuse into a chilled champagne flute, then, with a steady hand, gently pour in the triple sec to make a second layer.

2 Gently add the cherry brandy to make a third layer, the crème violette to make a fourth, the yellow Chartreuse to make a fifth, and the Curaçao to make a sixth.

3 Finally, float the brandy on top.

serves 1

measure chilled green Chartreuse

½ measure chilled triple sec

½ measure chilled cherry brandy

½ measure chilled crème violette

• ½ measure chilled yellow Chartreuse

• ½ measure chilled blue Curaçao

• ½ measure chilled brandy

This cocktail is named in honor of Maximum
Dog, who is himself a cocktail of breeds and who
has been described as a cross between a goat
and a monkey. However, he is not
allowed to drink it.

mad dog

serves 1

- 4–6 cracked ice cubes
- 1 measure white tequila
- 1 measure crème de banane
- 1 measure white crème de cacao
- ½ measure lime juice
- slice of lime, slice of banana, cocktail cherry, to decorate

1 Put the cracked ice cubes into a cocktail shaker. Pour the tequila, crème de banane, crème de cacao, and lime juice over the ice. Shake vigorously until a frost forms.

2 Strain into a chilled cocktail glass and decorate the glass with a lime slice, banana slice, and cocktail cherry.

jade

You can tell good jade because it always feels cold to the touch—and that should apply to cocktails, too. No cocktail bar—whether in a hotel, pub, or at home—can ever have too much ice. Don't forget to chill the champagne for at least 2 hours before mixing.

serves 1

- 4–6 cracked ice cubes
- dash of Angostura bitters
- ¼ measure Midori
- ¼ measure blue Curaçao
- ¼ measure lime juice
- chilled champagne, to top off
- slice of lime, to decorate

1 Put the cracked ice cubes into a cocktail shaker. Dash Angostura bitters over the ice and pour in the Midori, Curaçao, and lime juice. Shake vigorously until a frost forms.

2 Strain into a chilled champagne flute. Top off with chilled champagne and decorate with a slice of lime.

Both rum and bananas are naturally associated with the tropics, but wine does not spring so readily to mind when the Caribbean is mentioned. However, remember that France shares a long history with many Caribbean islands, such as Martinique and Guadeloupe.

caribbean
champagne

serves 1

- • ½ measure white rum
- • ½ measure crème de banane
- • chilled champagne, to top off
- • slice of banana, to decorate

1 Pour the rum and crème de banane into a chilled champagne flute. Top off with champagne.

2 Stir gently to mix and decorate with a slice of banana.

polynesian
pepper pot

It may seem strange to make a sweet drink and then season it with pepper and spices, but there is a long and honorable culinary tradition of making the most of the slightly acerbic flavor of pineapple in this kind of way.

serves

1

- 4–6 cracked ice cubes
- dash of Tabasco sauce
- 2 measures vodka
- 1 measure golden rum
- 4 measures pineapple juice
- ½ measure orgeat
- 1 tsp honey
- ¼ tsp curry powder
- pinch of curry powder

Put the cracked ice cubes into a mixing glass. Dash the Tabasco sauce over the ice and pour in the vodka, pineapple juice, orgeat, and lemon juice and add the honey. Shake

2

The traditional nuptial journey is so called because the first month of marriage was thought to be sweet—and why not? If you are sick of the sight of champagne following the wedding, why not share this sweet concoction?

honeymoon

serves 2

- 8–10 cracked ice cubes
- 4 measures apple brandy
- 2 measures Bénédictine
- 2 measures lemon juice
- 2 tsp triple sec

1 Put the cracked ice cubes into a cocktail shaker. Pour the brandy, Bénédictine, lemon juice, and triple sec over the ice. Shake vigorously until a frost forms.

2 Strain into two chilled cocktail glasses.

Nonalcoholic
Cocktails

lip smacker

This drink's delicious ingredients are
not just any healthy nonalcoholic
cocktail—they have come into their
own. Discover the kick of an
alcohol cocktail.

serves 1

• 4–6 cracked ice cubes

• 1 small tomato, peeled,
  seeded, and chopped

• 1 measure orange juice

• 2 tsp lime juice

• 1 scallion, chopped

• 1 small fresh red chile,

1 Put the cracked ice cubes, tomato,
orange juice, lime juice, scallion, and
chile in a blender and process
until smooth.

2 Pour into a chilled glass, and stir
in the sugar, salt, and Tabasco sauce.
Decorate with a lime slice and a chile

Generally, the best nonalcoholic cocktails are originals rather than pale and often insipid copies of their traditional, alcoholic cousins. This nonalcoholic version of the Bloody Mary is one of the exceptions and has some of the kick of the classic cocktail.

bloody january

serves 1

- **4–6 crushed ice cubes**
- **1 medium red bell pepper, seeded and coarsely chopped**
- **2 large tomatoes, peeled, seeded, and coarsely chopped**
- **1 fresh green chile, seeded**
- **juice of 1 lime**
- **salt and freshly ground black pepper**
- **celery stalk, to decorate**

1 Put the crushed ice cubes into a blender and add the red pepper, tomatoes, chile, and lime juice. Blend until smooth.

2 Pour into a chilled highball glass and season to taste with salt and pepper. Decorate with a celery stalk.

carrot cream

Although vegetables, carrots have a strong hint of sweetness that makes them or their juice an excellent and delicious basis for mixed drinks. Since raw carrots are packed with vitamins and minerals, this is a healthy option, too.

serves 1

- 4–6 cracked ice cubes
- 2 measures carrot juice
- 2½ measures light cream
- 1 measure orange juice
- 1 egg yolk
- slice of orange, to decorate

1 Put the cracked ice cubes into a cocktail shaker. Pour the carrot juice, cream, and orange juice over the ice and add the egg yolk. Shake vigorously until a frost forms.

2 Strain into a chilled glass and decorate with the orange slice.

This is another good cocktail for a Sunday brunch, when alcoholic drinks can be too soporific and you end up wasting the rest of the day, but you still want something to wake up the taste buds and set them tingling.

clam digger

...es into a

...basco sauce

...ver the ice,

...d clam juice,

...ce. Shake

...ns.

...lass with

...the cocktail

...with celery

...te with a

eye of the
hurricane

In recent years, a vast range of fruit juices and syrups has become widely available. These can extend the range of the cocktail bar and are particularly useful for nonalcoholic mixed drinks, which were once heavily dependent on the rather tired old favorites of orange, lemon, and lime juices.

serves 1

- 4–6 cracked ice cubes
- 2 measures passion fruit syrup
- 1 measure lime juice
- bitter lemon, to top off
- slice of lemon, to decorate

1 Put the cracked ice cubes into a mixing glass. Pour the syrup and lime juice over the ice and stir well to mix.

2 Strain into a chilled glass and top off with bitter lemon. Stir gently and decorate with the lemon slice.

faux kir

A nonalcoholic version of a classic wine cocktail, this drink is just as colorful and tasty. French and Italian fruit syrups are often the best quality and have the most intense flavor.

serves 1

- **1 measure chilled raspberry syrup**

- **chilled white grape juice, to top off**

- **twist of lemon peel, to decorate**

1 Pour the raspberry syrup into a chilled wine glass. Top off with the grape juice.

2 Stir well to mix and decorate with the lemon twist.

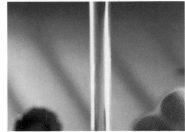

juicy julep

Taken from the Arabic word, meaning a rose syrup,
it seems likely that this was always intended to be a
nonalcoholic drink and that it was bourbon-drinkers
who hijacked the term, not the other way round.

serves 1

• 4–6 cracked ice cubes

• 1 measure orange juice

• 1 measure pineapple juice

• 1 measure lime juice

• ½ measure raspberry syrup

• 4 crushed fresh mint leaves

• ginger ale,
to top off

• fresh sprig of mint,
to decorate

1 Put the cracked ice cubes into
a cocktail shaker. Pour the orange
juice, pineapple juice, lime juice, and
raspberry syrup over the ice and add
the mint leaves. Shake vigorously until
a frost forms.

2 Strain into a chilled Collins glass,
top off with ginger ale, and stir gently.
Decorate with a fresh mint sprig.

110

Nothing could be more refreshing on a hot summer's day than this colorful combination of tropical fruit juices. To get into a party mood, go to town with the decoration.

and cooler

serves 1

- 8–10 cracked ice cubes
- 2 measures orange juice
- 1 measure lemon juice
- 1 measure pineapple juice
- 1 measure papaya juice
- ½ tsp grenadine
- sparkling mineral water, to top off
- pineapple wedges, cocktail cherries, to decorate

1 Put 4–6 cracked ice cubes into a cocktail shaker. Pour the orange juice, lemon juice, pineapple juice, papaya juice, and grenadine over the ice. Shake vigorously until a frost forms.

2 Half fill a chilled Collins glass with cracked ice cubes and pour the cocktail over them. Top off with sparkling mineral water and stir gently. Decorate with pineapple wedges and cocktail cherries speared on a cocktail stick.

little prince

Sparkling apple juice is a particularly useful
ingredient in nonalcoholic cocktails because
it adds flavor and color, as well as fizz. Try using
it as a substitute for champagne in
nonalcoholic versions of such cocktails as
Buck's Fizz (see page 59).

serves 1

- **4–6 cracked ice cubes**

- **1 measure apricot juice**

- **1 measure lemon juice**

- **2 measures sparkling apple juice**

- **twist of lemon peel,
  to decorate**

1 Put the cracked ice cubes
into a mixing glass. Pour the
apricot juice, lemon juice, and
apple juice over the ice and
stir well.

2 Strain into a chilled
highball glass and decorate
with the lemon twist.

Peach Melba was a dessert invented by Escoffier, chef at the Savoy Hotel in London, in honor of the Australian opera singer Dame Nellie Melba. This simple, but perfect partnership of peaches and raspberries has become a classic combination, now transformed into a wonderfully refreshing cocktail.

sparkling
peach melba

serves 1

- ¼ cup frozen raspberries
- 4 measures peach juice
- sparkling mineral water, to top off

1 Rub the raspberries through a wire strainer with the back of a wooden spoon, then transfer the purée to a cocktail shaker.

2 Pour the peach juice into the cocktail shaker and shake vigorously until a frost forms.

3 Strain into a tall, chilled glass and top off with sparkling mineral water. Stir gently.

california
smoothie

Smoothies of all sorts—alcoholic and nonalcoholic—have become immensely popular in the last two or three years. The secret of success is to blend them on medium speed until just smooth.

serves 1

- **1 banana, peeled and thinly sliced**
- **½ cup strawberries**
- **½ cup pitted dates**
- **4½ tsp honey**
- **1 cup orange juice**
- **4–6 crushed ice cubes**

1 Put the banana, strawberries, dates, and honey into a blender and blend until smooth.

2 Add the orange juice and crushed ice cubes and blend again until smooth. Pour into a chilled Collins glass.

Available from Italian delicatessens and some supermarkets, Italian syrup comes in a wide variety of flavors, including a range of fruit and nuts. French syrups are similar and also include many different flavors. You can substitute your favorite for the hazelnut used here and vary the quantity depending on how sweet you like your drinks to be.

italian soda

serves 1

- **6–8 cracked ice cubes**
- **1–1½ measures hazelnut syrup**
- **sparkling mineral water, to top off**
- **slice of lime, to decorate**

1 Fill a chilled Collins glass with cracked ice cubes. Pour the hazelnut syrup over the ice and top off with sparkling mineral water.

2 Stir gently and decorate with the lime slice.

grapefruit
cooler

This is a wonderfully refreshing drink that
is ideal for serving at a family barbecue.
Start making this at least four hours
before you want to serve it to allow plenty
of time for the mint to infuse in the syrup.

serves 6

- **2 oz/55 g fresh mint**
- **2 measures sugar syrup (see page 15)**
- **2 cups grapefruit juice**
- **4 measures lemon juice**
- **about 30 cracked ice cubes**
- **sparkling mineral water,
  to top off**
- **sprigs of fresh mint
  to decorate**

1 Crush the fresh mint leaves and
place in a small bowl. Add the sugar
syrup and stir well. Set aside for at
least 2 hours to macerate, mashing the
mint with a spoon from time to time.

2 Strain the syrup into a pitcher
and add the grapefruit juice and lemon
juice. Cover with plastic wrap and let
chill in the refrigerator for at least
2 hours, until required.

3 To serve, fill six chilled Collins
glasses with cracked ice. Divide the
cocktail between the glasses and top
off with sparkling mineral water.
Decorate with fresh mint sprigs.

A sophisticated, nonalcoholic punch, this
can be served chilled for a summer party.

cranberry punch

serves 10

- 2½ cups cranberry juice
- 2½ cups orange juice
- ⅔ cup water
- ½ tsp ground ginger
- ¼ tsp ground cinnamon
- ¼ tsp freshly grated nutmeg
- cracked ice cubes or block of ice

- fresh cranberries,
1 egg white, lightly beaten,
superfine sugar,
sprigs of fresh mint,
to decorate

1 First prepare the decoration.
Dip the cranberries, one by one, in the
egg white and let the excess drip off,
then roll them in the sugar to frost,
shaking off any excess. Set aside on
parchment paper to dry. Brush the mint
leaves with egg white and then dip in
the sugar to frost, shaking off any excess.
Set aside on parchment paper to dry.

2 Put the cranberry juice, orange
juice, water, ginger, cinnamon, and
nutmeg in a pan and bring to a boil.
Reduce the heat and let simmer for
5 minutes.

3 Remove the pan from the heat
and set aside to cool. Pour into a
pitcher, cover with plastic wrap, and
let chill in the refrigerator for at least
2 hours, until required.

4 Place cracked ice cubes or a
block of ice in a chilled punch bowl
and pour in the punch. Alternatively,
fill glasses with cracked ice cubes
and pour the punch over them.
Decorate with the frosted
cranberries and mint leaves.

Definitely for people with a sweet tooth, this is a chocoholic's dream and is popular with adults, as well as children.

mocha slush

serves 1

- **4–6 crushed ice cubes**
- **2 measures coffee syrup**
- **1 measure chocolate syrup**
- **4 measures milk**
- **grated chocolate, to decorate**

1 Put the crushed ice cubes into a blender and add the coffee syrup, chocolate syrup, and milk. Blend until slushy.

2 Pour into a chilled goblet and sprinkle with grated chocolate.

This is one of the most famous of classic nonalcoholic cocktails. Shirley Temple Black became a respected diplomat, but this cocktail dates from the days when she was an immensely popular child film star in the 1930s.

shirley temple

serves 1

- 8–10 cracked ice cubes
- 2 measures lemon juice
- ½ measure grenadine
- ½ measure sugar syrup (see page 13)
- ginger ale, to top off
- slice of orange, cocktail cherry, to decorate

1 Put the cracked ice cubes into a cocktail shaker. Pour the lemon juice, grenadine, and sugar syrup over the ice and shake vigorously.

2 Half fill a small, chilled glass with cracked ice cubes and strain the cocktail over them. Top off with ginger ale. Decorate with an orange slice and a cocktail cherry.

soft sangria

This is a version of the well-known Spanish wine cup that has caught out many an unwary tourist because it seems so innocuous, whereas it is actually very potent. A Soft Sangria poses no such danger of unexpected inebriation, but is just as refreshing and flavorsome. Make sure all the ingredients are thoroughly chilled before mixing.

serves 20

- **6 cups red grape juice**
- **1¼ cups orange juice**
- **3 measures cranberry juice**
- **2 measures lemon juice**
- **2 measures lime juice**
- **4 measures sugar syrup (see page 15)**
- **block of ice**
- **slices of lemon, orange, and lime, to decorate**

1 Put the grape juice, orange juice, cranberry juice, lemon juice, lime juice, and sugar syrup into a chilled punch bowl and stir well.

2 Add the ice and decorate with the slices of lemon, orange, and lime.

Choose a very ripe, sweet-fleshed melon, such as a cantaloupe, for this lovely, fresh-tasting cocktail. This drink is perfect for sipping on a hot evening.

melon
medley

serves 1

- 4–6 crushed ice cubes
- ½ cup diced melon flesh
- 4 measures orange juice
- ½ measure lemon juice

1 Put the crushed ice cubes into a blender and add the diced melon. Pour in the orange juice and lemon juice. Blend until slushy.

2 Pour into a chilled Collins glass.

121

cocktail glossary

Amaretto: almond-flavored liqueur from Italy

Amer Picon: French apéritif bitters, flavored with orange and gentian

Angostura bitters: rum-based bitters from Trinidad

Anisette: French liqueur, flavored with anise, cilantro, and other herbs

Applejack: North American name for apple brandy (see Fruit Brandy)

Aquavit: Scandinavian grain spirit, usually flavored with caraway

Armagnac: French brandy produced in Gascony—it is rarely used for cocktails

Bacardi: leading brand of white rum, originally from Cuba and now produced in Bermuda—also the name of a cocktail

Bailey's Irish Cream: Irish, whiskey-based, chocolate flavored liqueur

Bénédictine: French, monastic liqueur flavored with herbs, spices, and honey

Bitters: a flavor-enhancer made from berries, roots, and herbs

Bourbon: American whiskey made from a mash that must contain at least 51 percent corn

Brandy: spirit distilled from fermented grapes, although many fruit brandies are based on other fruits (see Fruit brandy)

Calvados: French apple brandy from Normandy

Campari: Italian bitters flavored with quinine

Champagne: French sparkling wine from La Champagne, produced under strictly controlled conditions

Chartreuse: French monastic liqueur flavored with a secret recipe of herbs—green Chartreuse is stronger than yellow

Cobbler: long, mixed drink traditionally based on sherry but now made from spirits and other ingredients

Coconut liqueur: coconut-flavored, spirit-based liqueur—Malibu is the best-known brand

Coffee liqueur: coffee-flavored, spirit-based liqueur—Tia Maria, based on Jamaican rum, and Kahlúa from Mexico are the best-known brands

Cointreau: best-selling brand of triple sec (see Triple sec), flavored with sweet Mediterranean oranges and Caribbean bitter orange peel

Collins: a spirit-based cocktail topped off with a carbonated soda, such as ginger ale

Crème de banane: banana-flavored liqueur

Crème de cacao: French, chocolate-flavored liqueur, produced in various strengths and colors

Crème de cassis: black currant-flavored liqueur, mainly from France

Crème de framboise: raspberry-flavored liqueur

Crème de menthe: mint-flavored liqueur—may be white or green

Crème de noyaux: liqueur made from apricot and peach pits

Crème violette: violet-flavored liqueur

Crème Yvette: American Parma violet-flavored liqueur

123

Curaçao: orange-flavored liqueur, produced mainly in France and the Netherlands, but originating from the Caribbean—available in a range of colors including white, orange, and blue

Drambuie: Scotch whisky-based liqueur, flavored with honey and heather

Dry gin: see Gin

Dubonnet: wine-based apéritif, flavored with quinine—available red and blonde

Eau-de-vie: spirit distilled from fruit—tends to be used (wrongly) as interchangeable with fruit brandy

Falernum: Caribbean syrup flavored with fruit and spices

Fernet Branca: Italian liqueur with a bitter flavor

Fizz: long, mixed drink, based on spirits and made fizzy with club soda

Flip: spirit based, creamy mixed drink made with egg

Fruit brandy: strictly speaking, brandy is distilled from fermented grapes, but many fruit brandies are distilled from whatever the fruit type is, such as apple and apricot—plum brandy, also known as slivovitz, is usually made from Mirabelle and Switzen plums

Galliano: Italian liqueur, flavored with honey and vanilla

Genever: also known as Hollands or Dutch gin, the original gin, which is sweeter and fuller-flavored than London, Plymouth, or dry gin—rarely used in cocktails (see Gin)

Gin: a colorless, grain-based spirit, strongly flavored with juniper and other herbs. London, Plymouth, and dry gin are most commonly used for cocktails

Gomme syrup: sweet syrup from France

Grand Marnier: French, orange flavored, Cognac-based liqueur

Grappa: fiery, Italian spirit distilled from wine must

Grenadine: nonalcoholic, pomegranate-flavored syrup—used for sweetening and coloring cocktails

Irish whiskey: unblended spirit made from malted or unmalted barley and some other grains—suitable for many cocktails

Julep: originally a sweet syrup, now a family of spirit-based cocktails, flavored and decorated with fresh mint

Kahlúa: popular Mexican brand of coffee liqueur

Kirsch: colorless cherry-flavored eau-de-vie, mainly from France and Switzerland

Kümmel: colorless Dutch liqueur, flavored with caraway

Lillet: French herb-flavored liqueur, based on wine and Armagnac

Liqueur: distilled spirit flavored with such things as fruit, herbs, coffee, nuts, mint, and chocolate

London gin: the driest gin (see Gin)

Madeira: fortified wine from the island of the same name

Malibu: leading brand of coconut liqueur—based on rum

Mandarine Napoléon: Belgian, brandy-based liqueur flavored with tangerines

Maraschino: Italian, cherry-flavored liqueur—usually colorless, but may be red

Martini: popular Italian brand of vermouth produced by Martini and Rossi and also the name of a classic cocktail

Melon liqueur: spirit-based, melon-flavored liqueur—Midori is the leading brand

Midori: Japanese liqueur (see Melon Liqueur)

Noilly Prat: leading French brand of very dry vermouth

Orgeat: almond-flavored syrup

Pastis: anise-flavored liqueur from France

Plymouth gin: a less dry type of gin than London gin (see Gin)

Port: Portuguese fortified wine that may be white, ruby, or tawny—white and Inexpensive ruby are most appropriate for cocktails

Pousse-café: a drink poured in layers to float on top of one another, which gives its name to a narrow, straight-sided stemmed glass

Quinquina: French, wine-based apéritif, flavored with quinine

Rickey: a spirit-based cocktail including lemon or lime juice and club soda

Rum: spirit distilled from fermented sugar cane juice or molasses—light, golden, and dark have distinctive flavors and all are widely used, together and severally, in cocktails and punches

Rye whiskey: mainly American and Canadian whiskey which must be made from a mash containing at least 51 percent rye

Sake: Japanese rice wine

Sambuca: Italian, licorice-flavored liqueur

Schnapps: grain-based spirit—available in a range of flavors, including peach and peppermint

Scotch whisky: blends are a mixture of about 40 percent malt and 60 percent grain whisky and are most suitable for cocktails—single malts should be drunk neat or diluted with water

Slammer: a cocktail mixed by slamming it on the bar

Slivovitz: plum brandy (see Fruit Brandy)

Sloe gin: Liqueur made by steeping sloes in gin—previously homemade but now available commercially

Sour: a spirit-based cocktail containing sugar, and lemon or lime juice

Southern Comfort: American whiskey-based, peach-flavored liqueur

Strega: Italian, herb-flavored liqueur

Sugar syrup: a sweetener for cocktails, made by dissolving sugar in boiling water (see page 15)

Swedish Punch: aromatic rum-based drink, flavored with wines and syrups

Tequila: Mexican spirit distilled from pulque from fermented maguey cacti

Tia Maria: popular, Jamaican rum-based coffee liqueur

Triple sec: colorless, orange-flavored liqueur

Vermouth: wine-based apéritif flavored with extracts of wormwood—both sweet and dry vermouths are widely used in cocktails

Vodka: colorless, grain-based spirit, originally from Russia and Poland. Flavored vodkas, such as lemon, raspberry, and chili, are becoming increasingly popular

Whiskey: spirit distilled from grain or malted barley—the main types are bourbon, rye, Irish, and Scotch

cocktail index